God Ain't Sleep

Yesterday, Today and Tomorrow

JUDI MOORE LATTA

Carolyn Wilcox —
Continue to tell
your story and make
a difference in the
lives around you.
Be blessed!

J Latta
10/30/2015

God Ain't Sleep – Yesterday, Today and Tomorrow
Copyright © 2015 by Judi Moore Latta

Printed in the United States of America
First Printing, 2015

ISBN-13:
978-1515325390

ISBN-10:
1515325393

Editor: Raven Padgett

Cover design by Vikiana

Cover photograph by Kerry-Ann Hamilton:
Cadillac Mountain (in Acadia National Park, Maine) is the highest point along the North Atlantic seaboard and the first place to see sunrise in the United States during several months of the year.

<u>**Dedication**</u>

For *Joe*, who loved me through many of the experiences in this book and listened to every word in these stories multiple times.

For *Mom and Dad*, who continue to smile.

Contents

Acknowledgments

Introduction   3

1.   What Cancer Taught Me about Love   5

2.   "God Ain't Sleep"   11

3.   The Gospel According to Aunt Mae   17

4.   Lesson on Calhoun Street   21

5.   The Shed in Oak Knoll   25

6.   The Gatekeeper's Apprenticeship   31

7.   Take the Risk, Bite the Elephant   35

8.   The Potter and the Clay   41

9.   More Than A Few Good Men   43

10.   No Red Light in Ty Ty   47

11.   An Open Letter to Our Grandson Little John on Turning 18   49

12.   A Few Final Thoughts   51

A Note on the Author   53

<u>Acknowledgments</u>

These stories tumbled out and took shape in a concentrated period of time. I am grateful to my husband Joe Latta who propped me up with love and prayers, patiently granted me space to write and gently pushed me forward.

I thank God for Dackeyia Simmons Sterling, who once was my student and now I am hers. For contributions at their highest professional levels, I thank Raven Padgett (my editor), Kerry-Ann Hamilton (cover photo), Jason Miccolo Johnson (author photo), Linda Wharton Boyd, Ashley Bayton, TaJuan "TeeJ" Mercer and Ingrid Sturgis.   Many thanks to other friends who generously offered wisdom in one way or another on this project. Some read or heard versions of chapters and gave their insights. Among them: Vicci Saunders, Pam Ferrell, Wanda Ferrell and Alfred Smith. I also thank those referenced in these stories: Mel Cummings who shared much of the journey; Dianne Boardley Suber who gave me the elephant; marvelous physicians –Drs. Lori Wilson, E. Cooke-Sampson, J. Dunmore-Griffith, O. Filani and Wayne Frederick; master cleaner Fred Charles Hadley; Elbert Wilson from Ty Ty; my Grandson John; and Ellis Gordon, Jr. who reminded me to tell.

Others from our close-knit community additionally have been there for me, sometimes without knowing it: my uncle Thomas Entzminger; my children Nikole Duppins, Lauren Mangrum and John Mangrum; other "sisters and brothers by claim," including Jacqui Malone, Freeman and Jackie Hrabowski, Hansel and Paula Tookes, Darryl Tookes, JoAnn and Phil Mussenden, Bishetta Merritt, Gladys Gary Vaughn; Rev. Donald Kelly, Brenda Kelly and the Olive Branch Community Church family including particularly Tina

Mance Lee, Effie Macklin, Jackie and Cliff Slay, Carla Malone, Crystal Wilson, and Doris Howard. Others have given ongoing support including media friends Raki Jones, Sandra Rattley, Adam Powell, Jim Watkins and Jeff Lee. I share a special bond with the D.C. Divas, my Howard University colleagues and my Florida community—Altha Manning, Doby Flowers, the Flowers clan, Larry and Dorothy Hunt and Ronald Belton.

I am particularly grateful to Wil Haygood, Sonja Williams and Cheryl LaRoche. Wil showed me the potential of a single voice. Sonja and Cheryl invited me to explore the beauty of a single perspective as part of the non-fiction writers Tuesday group, which includes Nancy Derr, Michael Scadron, Michael Kirkland, Diana Parsell, Bonny Miller and Ken Ackerman.

I'm grateful to many more whose names are in my heart. I thank God for all of them and for the will to take the journey.

www.GodAintSleep.com

Introduction

My mother LaVerne Moore, a colored teacher in the segregated South, was the daughter of Cornelia Jackson, a domestic worker in the pretend-not-to-be segregated North, who was the daughter of Julia Hand, found abandoned in a cornfield in Ohio in the mid-1800s. There's something about this lineage that makes me whole, a child of Grace.

I can barely remember Mama giving me the note that I stashed in the back of my wallet. I put it there and forgot it. Mama, with her teacher's sensibility and her penchant for saving money, hand wrote notes as if writing them ensured that future readers would avoid making mistakes or being misguided. She wrote notes to help—recipes she found in obscure places, warnings for appliances that were quirky and difficult to use, a directory on the freezer door of what frozen foods to find on the three shelves. Everything was fair game as Mom's notes appeared everywhere in her house and mine as some form of preparation.

So it is remarkable that I recall her saying, "You might need this one day," as I tucked her handwritten Post-it size note in the back of my wallet, waiting to be transferred each year to a new holder. *Out of sight, out of mind* was my mantra.

Seven years after Mama died, the note appeared, faded and crumpled. On a day that was particularly hard, it surfaced. I was feeling alone and despondent, having just received a medical diagnosis that frightened me. Under attack from an enemy; a victim singled out for attention, I thought. And as if my mother spoke from the grave, the note with frayed edges fell out of my wallet.

No tears are shed that God does not notice. ...[He] is not perplexed by the multiplicity of cares or overwhelmed by their weight... In the daily changes taking place around us, we are able to find precious lessons, if our hearts are open to discern them.

She had copied the words from someone somewhere. I later learned it was a quote from Ellen G. White about a journey in faith. In the midst of a most difficult time for me, these words served as a reminder.

Years ago I heard someone casually quip, "God Ain't Sleep," and I *felt* what he meant, but I didn't *know* for sure. I knew God was omnipotent but I had never really thought about sleep. Not until I had my personal proof did I understand that God connects to the smallest tears, presides over the tiniest moans, leads in the most unlikely directions, guides the most hesitant steps, pushes the greatest boundaries and makes the impossible happen everyday.

The thought that God takes notice has been the motivation for this gathering of real life stories. For years before and since Mama died I have been writing, knowing unconsciously, like my foremothers, I'm in God's hands, but sometimes forgetting that my daily surroundings are evidence. We all need encouragement and reminders. The enemy cannot triumph. This book offers some personal moments from yesterday that I have learned about today. These are poured out as "precious lessons" I've witnessed about friendship, faith and love in preparation for tomorrow.

If you've ever made a mistake, felt overwhelmed, considered quitting, abandoned hope, needed encouragement to follow a dream, questioned God, then read on. You need this book. In your search for balance and perspective, you may find your own moments when you realize, "God ain't sleep."

1

What Cancer Taught Me about Love

Mid-February, 2015

It was no accident that the physician gave me his personal cell. This was my second routine checkup with him and I reminded him how much I missed my previous doctor, who had recently announced his retirement. The new, young replacement tried hard to please and did a good job. "Call if you ever need anything," he said. Shoving into my hand his card with his handwritten phone number on the back, he whispered, "Just in case." A week later as I did a self-exam in the shower, I felt the lump in my left breast and knew something wasn't right. I called.

Within 24 hours I found myself back in his office and within hours of that, as the last patient on a Friday night, in the women's imaging center having a mammogram. The technician doing the procedure smiled enough but chattered on about her son's school problems. Preoccupied with her boy's troubles, she seemed oblivious to my breast being mashed into place on the cold machine. I tried to help—both with the positioning of my body and advice for her son. I gave her names and tips she might try, programs she might consider and my best professional academic advice in between trying to hold my breath and follow her instructions. She seemed grateful—encouraged, in fact—and thanked me profusely.

After the pictures, in a move quite out of the ordinary, she asked me to wait. "Do you have a few minutes?" she said, as if saying, "Thank you for your advice." She ran out of the exam room to get the physician on duty. A woman I had not met before came in, took a look at the images on the screen, squeezed her eyes and lips tight and told me, "I need to call your primary physician on Monday morning."

"I have his number now," I said, pulling the crumbled card from my purse for this "Just in case" moment. She took it and within minutes I was scheduled for a biopsy the next day.

The rest is a whirlwind. "It's cancer." I can't remember exactly when I heard the dreaded words, but I do remember asking, "Are you sure?" The tears lasted only a moment. I could hear my girlfriends even before they said it, "God's got this." The tests proceeded—MRI, PET-CT scans, X-rays and others I did not know by name. Sliding in and out of machines that entombed me and required me not to move proved difficult but not as difficult as hearing the outcome. Invasive ductile carcinoma. The diagnosis sounded ominous.

Having your mortality flash in front of your eyes is enough to make you stop in your tracks. Even a mind that usually races ahead to see what the end's going to be comes to a crawl. Images and thoughts pass with the smooth agility of a digital film in slow motion. Crisp, clear and sharp. Every frame moves like cells and molecules gathering to celebrate. You notice people. You search faces and bodies for clues before words come out. When a surgical team gathers, are there smiles? When a radiation therapist enters an exam room with news of whether an anticipated treatment will work, does she have a skip in her walk?

You notice things you never saw or wanted to see before and you appreciate relationships in a new way.

My surgeon was a blessing. When I first met Dr. Lori Wilson, who led my team at Howard University Hospital, she answered every question and never took her eyes off of me for the full first hour we talked. She anticipated my fears, projected my thoughts and described what I would feel in my body, my mind and my spirit.

When we talked, her eyes held mine and wouldn't let go, as if she could rescue me from any bottomless pit I thought I might find. She was a Godsend. But it wasn't until after the surgery that I realized why I could feel her soul. She is a survivor.

Personally struck by two different forms of breast cancer in the midst of an emerging career as an oncologist and cancer center administrator, she is compassionate beyond words. Her story, featured in the Ken Burns documentary series *Cancer: Emperor of All Maladies*, tells of a brilliant surgeon who has the hands of a sculptor and the heart of an angel. She is the one who cut the malignancy from my breast.

When my husband Joe and I took our vows, we promised to "love and cherish" … "for better or for worse …in sickness and in health…" and we really believed what we said. We have lived the vows. But not until my diagnosis did I understand the depth of my husband's commitment, the reach of his promise and the power of his love.

A marriage can be tested in many ways but the "in sickness and in health" part presents the biggest test. It's when one partner is not pretty or lovable or happy or quick to smile or able to fix meals or able to follow a regular independent routine. It's when getting up each day is a challenge and holding on to hope is a dream. It's when aches and pains become the utterances and helplessness the norm. It's when you have no idea of what the outcomes will be nor what the inputs can handle. It's at moments like these that faith kicks in and God shows out.

The week following my surgery was difficult as I prepared for the second stage of my treatment. My medical team had placed a stent in my chest in anticipation of a radiation therapy they thought might work. Simulations and follow-ups proved that wasn't the best approach, but not before a week of challenges. During that time, Joe made me feel special. He went to doctor's appointments with me, stood by for difficult procedures, asked every imaginable question and used his recorder to document what physicians said so we could discuss later. He chauffeured and coddled me and when I was at my lowest, he prayed.

Love too took the form of a village and, sure enough, one friend called and said, "God's got this." My daughters were there checking regularly. As an only child, I don't have much blood family but my brothers-and-sisters "by claim" reminded me in a collective voice through their texts and visits, prayers and air kisses that friendship, laced with love, is irreplaceable.

On a day when I barely had the strength to move, the doorbell rang and my sister-neighbor rolled in a cart full of healthy organic groceries for me and some goodies for Joe, carefully labeled. "The wine is for you," she told him as she pulled out a bottle and what seemed like an endless stream of special treats for a week. Right behind her, another sister-friend brought soups and salad and a third shared her signature salmon and shrimp. Food became a gathering point, while my waning appetite was a reminder that I needed to eat healthier.

"*Eat to Live* is a good book to get," one friend advised. Being intrigued by the title, I bought it immediately, bravely working my way through its recipes for kale smoothies and green shakes. "Cancer doesn't like green," somebody told me and I became a fanatic, looking for two-pound bags of green vegetables.

I never realized how the little things that people do can make such a difference. My friends volunteered to teach my classes, to drive me to hair appointments, to complete a 5k leg of a walk for breast cancer in my name, to lift me in prayer circles. They phoned to say if I needed them they would come from Baltimore, Florida, Connecticut, California, Virginia and Massachusetts to help. They called once a week and sometimes every day; they sent notes and cards of encouragement, as well as flowers; they gave me names of other friends who'd been through similar ordeals and witnessed triumphs. They became my lifelines and never even realized it.

God Ain't Sleep

Friday, May 22, 2015, was special. It dawned on the same day as one of my girlfriend's birthday and the 107th anniversary of my late father's birth. My dad Oscar Moore had been gone for nearly 20 years but I knew he watched from above. I was still a Daddy's girl. On that day, I became a survivor. When I finished my last radiation treatment, the oncology team ceremoniously lined up and presented me with proof that I had done it. The paper-framed document had signatures from the radiation oncologist Dr. Jacquelyn Dunmore-Griffith and every member of the team who had smiled upon me during the weeks of treatment. One of the radiation therapists I had gotten to know well, called it a "Certificate of Courage." Another said, "This is graduation." I thought about the many people I know who have been and are going through this and even more intense treatment. I accepted the certificate for all of them.

Several weeks before I had received the results of my recent HER2 test, which detects abnormal cells. "No additional cancer in the lymph nodes; no cancer in the surrounding tissue." When Dr. Wilson gave me the news, the hallelujah shout broke out in my heart and my step. God is good. He is merciful.

Months later, as I reflect, I realize that the entire experience has been humbling. It has compelled me to go deeper—mentally, relationally and spiritually. My priorities have changed. Every test I've endured, every procedure I've watched from inside out, every friend I have met again for the first time, every moment has been precious. I'm grateful for new eyes. For however long and in whatever ways God has something more for me to do, I'm willing.

2

"God Ain't Sleep"

Airport shuttle bus drivers are wise. That may be because they see a parade of people slogging onto and off of their busses, luggage in tow, intent on a destination but no idea really about the journey. It may not be that they are clairvoyant, but because of their perch in the front of the bus with a rearview mirror for observing the hard-to-see, they witness things that others might miss.

My husband and I met a shuttle bus driver one humid summer morning in 2008 at 5:00 a.m., just before dawn in the parking lot at Baltimore-Washington International Airport. The night before a major storm with hurricane gale winds, one of the worst in half a decade to hit our region, had caused havoc throughout the area. Our drive to the airport had been treacherous, as we had scrambled past downed power lines and trees on dark streets not yet lit by the sun. It was two days ahead of the 4th of July weekend and we were worn out as we headed to a six-day respite in St. Thomas, Virgin Islands. Our flight was scheduled at 6:30 a.m. Sitting on the shuttle bus an hour and a half in advance in the parking lot, we thought we had plenty of time.

Since no one else sat on the bus, the driver engaged us in conversation. Pleasant and chipper and emboldened by a special kinship because we too were Black, he talked non-stop. From the moment we boarded, he waxed about the early morning high humidity, the stingy wages that came from the bus service owner, the merits of exercise and anything else that came to his mind. And then a question out of nowhere: "What do you think about what's happening to Obama?" he asked. He probed for a speculation from us on the public pummeling that candidate Barack Obama had received in the polls from the political right and left. Clearly, this driver was a fan, a supporter who saw a potential Obama victory as a personal triumph. But before we could even offer a thought, he gave his own measured response as if he had pinned it to the "wisdom tree" that so many Southern Black preachers referenced in their prayers. He assured us that no matter how dim prospects might seem for the candidate during the campaign season, he could feel the Divine at work. Something better lay ahead.

He concluded his soliloquy with a prediction. "God ain't sleep," he said. "God ain't sleep..." The words echoed in my head because they seemed right. I had no idea of how, but they seemed to apply to more than an election.

By the time we reached pre-boarding and check-in, things had started to unravel. First, the counter clerk insisted upon seeing our passports. And no matter how much we argued we didn't need them to travel to a U.S. territory, the clerk was unmoved.

"No passports, no travel," he said, planting his feet firmly in an I-will-not-be-moved stance that worried me and exasperated my husband. So early in the morning no supervisor-to-overrule was available. Our passports were at home in our bedroom drawer—20 miles away! Our long-awaited holiday fling, planned for a year, flashed fleetingly in front of us. It would be ruined unless one of us could go home, get the documents and get back before the plane left. We decided on the spot. We had air tickets, hotel reservations and dreams of a magical getaway. One hour stood between us and that. It was worth the try. Negotiating in our partnership, we pulled mental lots and decided that Joe would go. The mad dash began.

Out the terminal door he ran and "Voila!" The shuttle bus driver from before sat waiting, as if sent back to shepherd through his earlier promise of "God ain't sleep." But it seemed to me, in my pessimism, that God, at least, had dozed.

In the car and then 40 miles roundtrip at breakneck speed, Joe said he dodged weather-related obstacles and prayed all the way. Covering an impossible distance in record time, he moved. In the meantime, I kept watch at the terminal counter along with another passport-less traveler. She waited for hers to come from Pennsylvania so she could join her boyfriend to snorkel in Bonaire. When she learned she needed to have the document to travel, she had called a neighbor-friend in her apartment building, who jumped in his car to drive it across the miles and the state line to the Maryland airport.

The passport-less woman and I both waited, shifting nervously. She was in her early 20s; I was three times her age. She was white; I am Black. She was single; I am married. We, indeed, were different. But at that moment, we had a common need. Adversity in shared experiences makes strange bedfellows. The minutes ticked. A half hour went by. Then, 15 minutes before the plane's scheduled departure, the passports arrived. First Joe burst through the terminal door with ours; then on his heels, the traveler's friend came with hers. God wasn't sleep.

The three of us dashed into line, as though whipped there by fate. An airline employee—ironically in a red coat, dressed for the nay-saying business—met us head on. All he needed was horns.

"You won't be able to make this," he soured. "You're too late." We knew, however, that a missed flight in Baltimore meant probable disaster for the long run since we needed to make connections in Atlanta. Holidays were unforgiving and did not lend themselves to easy make-up arrangements. Flying stand-by would be a nightmare.

"Let's try for the plane," the now passported-woman said, as she convinced the Red Coat to rush the three of us to our departure point. Running as fast as we could through the terminal, with the

Red Coat complaining all the way, we hit the security line and stopped in our tracks. There was no rushing the federally-mandated process of checking everyone planning to fly. In defeat, we started to turn and head back to the main desk just as an airline angel from the ranks of the skycaps reminded us, "As long as the flight is still at the gate, there's hope."

We waited in line to pass through security. Shoes off. Laptops out. Impatiently, we shifted as folks in front took their time loading belongings on the security check conveyor belt as if at a farmer's market leisurely examining organic vegetables. No one ever seems to be in a hurry at a local co-op. The process seemed to drag. Finally done. In partial sprint, we three ran past the descending gates 8, 7, 6… and approached the departure point. Almost there, we could see our plane through the window. In fact, we could almost touch it. Then the Delta 747 in its full aeronautical splendor pushed slowly back from Gate #3. We had missed it.

The gate agent could feel our pain, especially since we wore it on our faces and in our "wait, wait" in unison. She consoled, "There'll be another." Only half convinced herself that there would be room for us on the next fully-booked flight, she signed us up for stand-by.

What followed took us on a roller coaster ride of ups and downs, orchestrated by a carnival operator we couldn't see. We played our part and when the stand-by seats available on the next flight totaled three, we took them. This plane was scheduled to reach Atlanta 10 minutes before our all-important connecting flight to St. Thomas would be leaving. Although our newfound acquaintance had more time to make her connection, we wondered if we could make ours. Could we run through Atlanta's Hartsfield-Jackson Airport and arrive at our gate in time after we landed? It would be tight, but a "yes" answer seemed plausible until reality hit. We were on the plane but were seated, of all places, in the very last row. We would have to wait until everyone else got off.

We said a quick prayer and concocted a scheme: tell the flight attendant our plight; ask her to ask those aboard to stay seated while we ran through the aisle; dash the 15 gates to the right place. Sounded like a solid plan. While we were still flying, the attendant made the announcement, of sorts, but evidently with not the right amount of conviction. On the ground, the moment the captain turned off the "fasten seat belt" sign, the entire plane jumped up. All 185 people on board stood between us and our dream vacation. We missed the connection by minutes.

The gate in Hartsfield was littered with dozens of anxious travelers, some waiting for planes not yet arrived, but a contingency in limbo for planes that had just left. The place was crowded, with no seats in the waiting area. I was discouraged. A pleasant enough woman with a Jamaican accent sat sprawled across two seats, surrounded by more carry-ons than seemed allowed.

"You might as well take it easy," she said, sensing our disappointment at missing the flight. "I've been on stand-by to St. Thomas for three days."

My heart sank further. We would never get there. There remained only one more Delta flight scheduled for the day and it was overbooked. No others would fly until after the holiday. We resigned ourselves to be added to the long list of stand-bys. In the meantime, what about other options? Other airlines? Other connections through different cities? Other countries, even? We thought about everything we could afford, exhausted the "Information Desk Help" and prayed. Nothing was available or, if it was, we reasoned it made no sense for us.

Not wanting to spend the 4th of July in the airport, we were about to give up. Who did we know in Atlanta? Would it make sense to stay there or should we try to rent a car and drive to Tallahassee or take a bus back home to Maryland? Sometimes, when your back is against the wall, you abandon hope and make "hungry" decisions. You are tempted to allow an empty belly growling for sustenance to guide your choices. Not a belly hungry for food, but one in need of an answer. In such a case, you conform and go along with a course because it's easiest.

We told our story a thousand times to anyone who would listen. Then a blessing happened. Calmly, an airline worker passing by, who had just met us, whispered casually, "You will make it on board this last flight." She wore her uniform as confidently as she spoke, reassuring us with the same authority as the shuttle bus driver we had met before dawn.

Within seconds, we heard another voice on the loud speaker, as if from heaven: "Joe and Judi Latta may board the plane."

I have no idea what happened; how we leapfrogged to the front of the line; what flight angels stood in our stead. But I do know we boarded, realizing we had just had a lesson in faith.

Most airport shuttle bus drivers really can see in rearview mirrors all the way to the back of the bus. What they see behind them informs what they know ahead. But they also see possibilities when none seem apparent. Whenever I'm in doubt in the future, I pray I will remember and will be able to tell somebody else when they need to know, hold on, because "God ain't sleep."

It took a while for me to process this and connect what happened on the trip to what the bus driver said. But when it clicked, I had an "a-ha moment" that changed my life! This is what my mother meant. Experiences don't have to be big or wide or deep to be worthy of God's notice. They don't have to be convoluted, complex or cracked. But if they are, that's OK. Our role is to pay attention to the "daily changes" and the "precious lessons" from them. God certainly does.

3

The Gospel According to Aunt Mae

When I first saw the little lady sitting in the nursing home, small fragile and staring, I had only an inkling of her brilliance. I had never met her but I had heard the stories from her family and my friends about how she had raised two boys—her sister's children—and made them into men the world was proud to know. She had wrestled opossum with her bare hands and prayed deacons from the local church under the table. In her not quite 5' 1" frame, she was a hero in Perry, Florida. Now at 105 years old, she sat with a smile on her miraculously wrinkle-free face. She wore no glasses and her eyes sometimes darted, but mostly stared.

Many in Perry called her "Aunt" (pronounced "Ain't") "Mae." Some simply called her "Mae." In a gigantic leap forward, a few of the town's white folks had come to call her "Mizz Jones." She had reached and passed the ultimate milestone of a century of living and had received proclamations and recognition from the mayor, the governor, her New Bethel Missionary Baptist Church family and the Boy Scouts. Even the NBC network affiliate anchor had flashed her photo on the morning air to say, "Congratulations, Ella Mae Jones."

Aunt Mae was from Barnesville, Georgia, but she had been living on the east side of Perry since she had married in the 1930s. She didn't live in the house now but she liked to think of the modest frame home that she loved as being nestled in the east, even if Perry was a "finger snap" town not big enough to have four sides. "Finger snap" was the way people driving in north Florida described the town. Why? From the time drivers saw the first sign for Perry on Highway I-10 to the time they saw the second, they could snap their fingers and have passed it.

I had heard the stories about Aunt Mae, like the one involving her husband, who most in their family called "Uncle." Once he had playfully derided her at a sacred prayer meeting. On the way to church that night, the two of them had had one of their moments and were not speaking when they arrived. Uncle, a usually pleasant man and a senior deacon, was in charge of the evening service. When it came time for the opening prayer, he announced loudly and with authority, "Pray, Mae." Without blinking an eye, and with just as much authority, she retorted, "Pray yourself!"

Then there was the story of how her adopted son Bob chose UCLA for graduate school in the early 1960s. The state of Florida, that at the time turned a blind eye to Black applicants, had promised that as long as he did not try to enroll in one of the predominantly white universities in the state, they would pay full tuition for him to attend any other university in the country. The University of California sounded like a good choice. So he went.

When he graduated and returned home, he announced that he had been "called to preach." Knowing how to read hearts as well as she could read phases of the moon, Aunt Mae, in her infinite wisdom, asked Bob, "Who called you to preach?" He thought for a moment, considered the source of his supplemental graduate fellowship, and answered, "Rockefeller." Aunt Mae, who believed in Bob's possibilities before he saw his own, quietly turned and in her signature gurgling voice, told him, "You need to forget it until the Lord calls you."

I had heard so many of the stories but I was totally unprepared for the barrage of wisdom that came from her words that day in the nursing home. For one hour my girlfriend Mel, who is her daughter-in-law, and I heard a lifetime of the gospel according to Aunt Mae.

When you've done a lot of living, you know how to make good use of time.

She painted her words with a palate blending the culture and history of a region. Her phrases were markers of memory that reached down deep into the promises and pain of her community. She talked about "can't-you-do, don't-you-try hair" and conjured up hot combs and tough "kitchens." These were the kinds of "kitchens" that lay at the nape of the necks of little Black girls as they sat between the legs of their mothers on a hair straightening mission, trying to hold their ears to avoid getting inadvertently burned by the comb.

Aunt Mae warned against nosiness and gave her recipe for being a good neighbor: "Six months to take care of my business and six months to leave yours alone." She talked about "sopping biscuits with syrup" and "cooking gopher, ashcake and hoghead cheese" in the ground. Dig the hole, build the fire, spread the ashes, bury the food, smolder and give it time. She said that when you do it right, it's so good it will "make you slap your mama but you better keep on running."

As she spoke, she conjured up for herself reminders of yesterday linked to enslaved ancestors she did not know by name, who "made due." Memory had been handed down and could not be interrupted even when others looked to appropriate it. She said, once a white lady tried. When the dinner guests raved about the meal they'd had, the white lady, who served as hostess, claimed personal credit for fixing it. The guests wanted details. As the lady stumbled through her lie, Aunt Mae, who had been the actual cook and the lady's maid for years, bristled. Under her breath she rattled off the ingredients and the steps. To herself she recalled the pain and the pleasure of handling the food. She knew the real answers to the questions and smirked with the secrets. "That lady didn't know nothing about cooking in the ashes," Aunt Mae told us.

One thought after another flowed, each causing us to smile and hinting at more than surface meanings. We noticed she had a tiny tear in the corner of one eye.

And then, as we gathered ourselves to leave, it was as if she knew we needed preparation for the unforgiving urban world we were about to re-enter. As if she could sense we needed to have a message to fortify us in tough times and hard places, she talked about "corn pone." She told us it was not the cornmeal and the salt, the lard nor the water that made a difference. None of the ingredients really made corn pone good. Neither was it the cast-iron cooking container that did it.

The power in the Southern delicacy that "made you want to raise your hand and testify" came from something else: where you place the skillet in relationship to the fire. The secret, Aunt Mae told us, to making good corn pone, is for it "to be *near* the fire rather than *in* it." That way you can get the full benefit of the warmth and not get burned. So it is in life.

Aunt Mae knew the way of the folk. On that day, I was glad she passed it on.

4

Lesson on Calhoun Street

Named for a hero of the Confederacy, Calhoun Street always had been one way. Since as long as I could remember, traffic moved in one direction along the moss-draped, tree-lined street in a lazy steady flow that reflected the pace of a city that didn't know it was under siege. Tallahassee in 1961 was that city. Calhoun embodied the conflict. It was one block over from the state capital buildings, lily white inside and out, and a few miles in either direction from two distinctively different institutions of higher learning: one Black; the other white. My mother was a respectable teacher at the former.

One trip to Calhoun Street with Mama taught me a lesson I've never forgotten. We drove downtown to pick up a few things and figured we were lucky to find a parking space on the one-way street. Folks who had cars jockeyed for space there because you could reach most of downtown on foot from anywhere within the few blocks that had parking. Mama eased our English Ford into the one available spot. This was the same five-in-the-floor, stick shift English Ford my Dad had taught me to drive at 13.

"Just in case," he said. As a Black family living in a small remote community outside of the city limits, we were vulnerable. Although I only drove practice runs on our street, my parents believed in being prepared.

"If anything ever happens to me when we're in the car," Mama had warned, "Take my pocketbook, the car keys and drive." She must have been focused on images of harassment from the White

Citizens Council or what some called, "the hunter's club." On this day, we were downtown and she drove.

We parked in front of one of the historic two-story houses on the street near a shop sporting head mannequins with a wide array of hats on sale. Brims and pillboxes, feathers and felt sat side-by-side, reminiscent of a fashion parade from television. Mama didn't wear hats much, or at least I don't recall her wearing anything other than the Florida A&M baseball caps Daddy brought home or the variety of sun visors she used in her physical education classes.

We walked the two blocks in the sticky heat to a dress shop on a nearby corner. It never seemed odd to me that we didn't try on any hats, shoes or dresses of any type in the shops along Calhoun. Only white people could do that. We'd walk right past the fashion plate mannequins and not blink. Mama made most of our dresses so I didn't have occasion to miss getting a fitting.

We stopped first to buy buttons and cloth and carried two bags of sewing supplies out of the fabric store. Then we headed to a dress shop to buy a sweater for me. She didn't knit so purchasing was the best option and off-season was the best time to buy because of the lower prices. (Mom searched for bargains.) A blue sweater caught her fancy and she put it over her left arm to look at others. Yellow was actually more becoming or the light green or my favorite, the white one with pink rosettes. Mama adroitly lifted the sweaters one at a time by the shoulders and pressed them against my back. It was the ingenuous way Black women had of measuring whether or not something would fit without violating the "no try on" rule. It preserved dignity while providing some measure of accuracy.

We decided on the white one. Mama went to the checkout counter as she explained to me how I could wear it with a number of things. As she talked, she pulled out her wallet, paid cash for the sweater and insisted that the clerk give her the change in her hand. White clerks commonly had a way of disrespecting Black customers by shoving change back toward them flat on the counter.

Nonverbally, it expressed their disdain for touching Blacks during the transaction. Whenever it happened to Mama, she would stand her ground and wait until the clerk picked up the money.

This particular clerk handed Mama the change in her hand and neatly folded the sweater, placing it in a bag. Out the door and down the street we sauntered, still talking. No hurry. We even took a moment to look again at the fabric store.

Finally, we reached the car parked on Calhoun. As Mama shifted the bag with the white sweater and the other bags, she reached for her car keys and noticed for the first time draped over her left arm, the blue sweater from the dress shop! Mama almost fainted. She shrieked. She had unintentionally walked out with the merchandise without paying for it. Without a thought, she grabbed me by the arm and practically flew the two blocks back to the dress shop, my feet barely touching the ground. Mortified, she muttered, "No, no, no," the whole way. She ran through the door, whipped around into the checkout line and stood nervously until her turn. She then pulled out eight one dollar bills and paid for the blue sweater.

I learned something that day. Mama could have put the bags in the trunk and driven away once we got to the car. After all, Black people never had been dealt a fair hand in the city and this might have been a way of shuffling the deck to make things even. Besides, no one had noticed her walking out of the store with the blue sweater and no one would have been the wiser about it missing. But Mama would have known. She believed in telling the truth, in being honest. So she left that day, her integrity intact and me in tow, and drove down Calhoun into my memory and my values.

❧

5

The Shed in Oak Knoll

Every Spring Break I went home to Tallahassee to look at the trees. It was my favorite pastime to escape the demands of students who pushed themselves to the limits and colleagues who wanted more of me than I could give. Oak Knoll offered a refuge. Spanish moss dangled naturally from four gigantic live oaks holding centuries of secrets too numerous to imagine. A shed, dwarfed by the shade, stood behind my childhood home as a reminder of possibilities.

The shed, plain and stoic, had been in the backyard some 60 years, at least since, as a little girl, I played "dolls and Mama" by myself, pretending to be grown. In those days I dared to dart into its dingy gloom only when necessary as Dad unlocked its door. In the shed he kept hammers and nails, rakes and clippers—all things that he "just might need some day" for his handiwork around the house. The shed cast its shadow inside and out and was the place I fancied goblins and figments of my imagination might dwell, like the dreaded fictitious "Miss Sugar," who haunted children's dreams. And although it did not invite play, it stayed on my mind for years as I looked at the trees. It always seemed to have a message.

On the spring day when I finally decided to take a look inside, I discovered that message. Decades of neglect had taken a toll. Rusted tools lay scattered on the shelves; rotten wood sat stacked in the corner; old paint had hardened and crusted over in cans kicked to the side. It was a mess! A limb from one of the oaks had fallen, perhaps some years before, and torn a gigantic hole in the roof. Months of rain and weather had come in. To my surprise, I could see everything. No dark gloom or shadowed crevices, no pitch black haunting presence like what I remembered. Instead, rays of sunshine beamed where the roof had been ripped completely off by a part of the tree that sat rotting in the corner. Light can be funny that way. Sometimes a limb destined to destroy, falls and allows in light so we can see things we couldn't see in a locked up dark space.

I knew immediately we needed a new shed! Like old habits and bad relationships, the old shed had to go. Like negative thoughts and shameful experiences, it needed to be history. "Get rid of this and start from scratch," I thought. We needed a place to house things and keep them, "just in case."

"Gotta call Fred Charles," I told my husband Joe, as I conjured up in my mind the best person I knew for the job, an expert in cleaning up messes. With all of his industrial strength apparatus, Fred Charles specialized in sanitizing office buildings and scouring old houses. It didn't take him long to tear down the shed and load the junk onto his flatbed. Soon, the old structure was gone and only a gaping space remained under the trees with little evidence that a shed had ever been there.

Fred Charles had a reputation for being good at what he did, so watching him hose down the ground did not seem unusual. For nearly three hours he swept and scrubbed, scraped and power-washed the leaves and the moldy earth in what looked like a fruitless rubbing. But soon something happened. There emerged a gleaming white floor, an 8 by 10 feet concrete foundation, solid as the day it was laid. It became clear to me at that moment that if you rub long and hard enough, you will reach a good foundation and have something on which you can build.

How hard could it be to build? Before we started, we should have asked anyone who has struggled in stealth to assemble a bicycle on Christmas Eve for a little one's wide-eyed surprise the next morning, especially if the directions were pictures.

Buying a prefab shed already built, complete with shingles, would have been easiest. But it would also have cost a fortune. Instead our best bet in the days remaining was to use the do-it-yourself approach that demanded a few tools, a little time and some patience. We had all three, I figured. So off to Lowe's. The label read, "Easy: you can do it!" but the fact that the box weighed a ton should have been the tip off. Getting help with moving it from the shelf of the hardware store to the back yard four miles away masked how difficult the task of building would be. When we finally maneuvered the "This side up" in the right direction and opened the carton, a thousand pieces stared at us, like a jigsaw puzzle. Completely overwhelmed, not knowing a screw from a bolt, we knew we needed help by step #2 of the building directions.

Tears welled up in my eyes as I considered that we had made a major mistake. Wrong choice. Should have gotten the prefab. Just then, a miracle drove into our driveway. "Master Carpenter" the side of the truck read. "Specialist in remodeling and wood rot removal." The man came because Fred Charles had called, anticipating this moment for us. Burly and brusque at more than six feet with a Southern drawl that reminded me of sugar cane, the master carpenter carried tools in the truck and a backup generator "just in case." My kind of man. He extended his hand in greeting; said his name was Raymond. I could tell he was the answer to a prayer. His hands were rough and used to hard work.

When you have only three days available and you're in trouble, there's nothing like being in good hands—hands that can build structures and change lives, pick up tools and give them a song, take what is common and make it special. Good hands can work miracles.

Raymond took the directions home, studied them for a night, came back the next day, meticulously laid out every piece and then began to follow the instructions. Like a virtuoso, he measured and placed, lifted and pounded as the shed took shape. Like a maestro conducting musicians or a choreographer   directing dancers, he put us both to work. Joe became the helper. I became the observer.

"I don't have a building bone in my body," I told the master carpenter.

He replied, "Yes you do. Everyone has."

"I can't build a thing," I retorted.

"You simply need to know how," he insisted.

"To build," he explained, "all you must do is remember four things: organize, square, level and plumb."

It was a life lesson. It made sense. I thought for a moment and flashed back 40 years to another precious moment in that same back yard. I was at my wit's end in the early 1970s trying to complete my master's degree and Mom gave me a book to read, simple and plain in its pages. *Jonathan Livingston Seagull* told the story of a bird with ambition, who heeded guidance to be better than ordinary. The words the wise gull told young Jonathan stuck with me for four decades: "To fly as fast as thought to anywhere that is, you must begin by knowing that you have already arrived." I finished the degree in a year and a half.

Same principle. Know from the start you can do it and you can fly. Believe at the beginning you can build and it will happen. Organize, square, level and plumb. The work on the shed seemed to roll out once the formula became clear. I could see, not only an end to the building, but lessons from the process itself.

If ever any advice had multiple levels, this was it. On the surface, Raymond the master carpenter said, "organize"; coordinate the parts. He meant for us to lay out nuts, bolts, nails and screws; assemble hammers and screw drivers on the grass; set up a step ladder next to the foundation; put numbered pieces of doors and handles, slabs and shingles side by side on the ground; and make sure the directions were prominently placed.

But his words went deeper. What if I organized my day, my work, my life? What if I disciplined what I ate, how much time I spent on choices, what priorities I held, the arrangement of my tools from prayer journal to computer? What powerful potential did I have to get set for a unified action?

The master carpenter said, take the next step and "square." He meant for us to use the principle of the 90-degree angle to make sure everything was in the right place so the building would not be crooked on its foundation. "A crooked building can't stand," he added.

Imagine testing your own upright position, where your right angles are in place. What you think matches what you say and what you say mirrors what you do. Imagine having principles and ideals that reflect your integrity and that earn you a reputation that screams justice.

Raymond the master carpenter explained the third step: "level."

"Make sure the horizontal perspectives are straight," he said.

I thought about it. In a building you can do it with an instrument. In a life you must do it with relationships: connecting with those you know in meaningful ways; showing that caring about those you don't know is more than a hashtag. Do you ask friends and family about having a mammogram or going for an overdue doctor's visit? Do you help a shut-in with a grocery run? Do you raise awareness about lost girls or hungry youth or abused women or anything beyond yourself? Does your emotional intelligence measure up to your intellect? Are your horizontal relationships level?

"The final step is plumb." Raymond finished the lesson. "That's looking at the vertical," he said, as he adroitly released a plumb line and let gravity do its work. Just as horizontal relationships mark the level, then vertical relationships mark the plumb. This is the last "must do" to make sure the structure stands in the way it was meant to stand.

My mind raced. I considered my verticals. Since I was born the great granddaughter of Julia, granddaughter of Cornelia, daughter of LaVerne, I had dropped like a plumb line from my ancestors in a vertical relationship with God. Despite tears here and there, that plumb had kept me grounded, guided and protected. A prayerful life and a belief in the Almighty have rooted me throughout my years. The vertical reached up and down; the horizontal reached from side to side. "That's the geography of the cross," I thought. What an amazing moment.

"Glad we didn't have to do nothing to the floor," Raymond's voice brought me back to the present. The shed looked good. 98 percent complete. The master carpenter and Joe were standing inside—one holding the door that swung back and forth while the other drove in the final screws to keep it in place. The floor beneath them was solid.

I don't know what would have happened had I not bothered to look inside the old shed when I did. Maybe it would have stayed there, locked up, housing its rusted secrets until they rotted away. Instead, in its place was a brand new shed built to hold tools "just in case." Who knows? In years to come a hurricane-size wind might blow it down or the Florida humidity might corrode it out. One day even, another generation might come to the shed in Oak Knoll and find a limb that's fallen through the roof. Regardless. What they are likely to find will be a good foundation. What I hope they will have will be a connection with a master carpenter who can show them how to build.

6

The Gatekeeper's Apprenticeship

I have always been unapologetic about learning. The full implication of that didn't occur to me, however, until I met Philip Simmons, an extraordinary craftsman. By the time he died at age 97, he had many names. People in Charleston called him a poet of iron, an artisan with a purpose, a living legend. In 1982, the National Endowment for the Arts recognized him as a National Heritage Fellow, the highest honor the country can bestow on a traditional artist. I would add that Philip Simmons was a master teacher.

I met him when I went on assignment from NPR to report on the African American material culture of South Carolina. Charleston served as the centerpiece of a long tradition of historic work whose influences stretched back to Africa and that neither the Middle Passage nor years in America had erased. I had heard that Mr. Simmons was in that tradition. He could make iron sing, make it look like a symphony sounded or like a village choir performed, working patterns and improvisations into each piece. He had molded and created more than 600 ornamental wrought iron works that guarded windows and graced homes as fences and gates. In short, he had worked for decades over his blacksmith's anvil, creating work that pleased residents and wowed visitors.

His story stretched back to another century when enslaved people had labored as blacksmiths, shipwrights and coopers and then taught others the craft. At the age of eight, he began learning about working iron and by 15 he had become a master at it. When I

31

met him, he was nearly 80 and the fire had become a part of his life. On the day our paths crossed, he worked in the backyard of his modest frame house on Blake Street almost playfully reaching into the fire of his forge with his bare hands. He was building a gate. With his hands appearing like an extra pair of tongs, he seemed to brush away any excess fire from the iron. Chocolate smooth skin glistening, he belied his nearly eight decades of life as he told stories.

"It looks like a leaf," he remarked as he began pulling the scrap out of the fire. I cautiously approached not wanting to disturb his concentration. Immediately I realized he fashioned the end of an ornate grate that appeared to blend a peacock's tail into a garden. The design shimmered through the fire. There were as many twists and turns as hidden parts made plain. Since it was the first piece of iron I had ever seen going through the process of being molded, I was amazed.

"I didn't intend to do it like this," he said, in heavily accented Gullah. His voice reminded me of my West Indian grandmother from Barbados. Bajans and Sea Islanders, after all, shared an immigration history from Africa. He talked about the gate emerging.

"In any other case," he continued, "this would have been an accident. But I don't believe in accidents." By now he had bent and pulled one of the small scraps so that it definitely looked like a leaf. He handed me this, his signature shape, as a stand-alone piece. "This is for you."

I took the small iron piece in my hands and felt instantly I was touching stories and history and genius all at once. The not-so-accidental leaf carried a message in its DNA. In this world, it said, accidents don't happen. While the intent might be for one purpose as something is in-the-works, its final use might be for something entirely different. It revealed that everything is part of a larger plan.

The afternoon with Mr. Simmons seemed to zip by. We talked about his life and his dreams, his memories and his view of the future. He told me about the man who had once been enslaved who had taught him to work iron with humility and skill; the same man who had showed him how to use the anvil like a musical instrument; the same man on Charleston's Calhoun Street who meshed the creative with the methodical; the same man who had helped him to see that accidents don't happen when you trust in the plan.

Just as the sun began to set and our interview ended, I went back to the beginning just to make sure I had all of the story straight.

"Mr. Simmons, how long were you apprenticed?"

Half expecting to hear him say a decade or less, I waited to confirm what I thought I knew. But Mr. Simmons dug down deeper than a number or a single person. He answered like one guarding passage through a precious gate. He stopped, put down the hammer and looked me directly in the eye.

"Apprenticed?" he said. "Apprenticed? I'm still apprenticed. I'm still learning."

There it was. A lesson I could not ignore. If this master craftsman, elder national treasure, saw himself as "still learning," then surely I must be doing the same. As long as I have breath, I hope that will be the case.

7

Take the Risk, Bite the Elephant

I'll tell you the truth. I never really wanted to go back to school after I'd finished. Being a student wasn't so bad but the first two times were enough, I thought, since what I really wanted to do in my career did not require an advanced degree. I boasted radio as my passion and telling stories as my commitment. I could do both whether or not I had a Ph.D. And besides, some folks said I was too old. I didn't dare to push back but others encouraged me. My husband, my parents, my friends—anticipating my progress teaching in the academy—all pressed me, saying some version of, "You never know what you might do, so just in case..."

The turning point came after I served as senior producer of *Wade in the Water: African American Sacred Music Traditions*, the 26-part cultural series for NPR and the Smithsonian Institution. It was the toughest research/production job I'd ever done, yet the project rocked with a dynamic team. When the series ended, I received a call that changed my life. A graduate student I didn't know randomly phoned to inquire about what she called, "the groundbreaking *Wade* process." Her questions fascinated me. We talked for an hour and I learned that she planned to use the content of the interview as the basis for a paper. At that moment, I decided that the story was good, but it was mine. If anybody should write this, it should be me. I hung up the phone and applied for the same program she claimed in American Studies.

The field suited me perfectly but I knew I would be older than most of my classmates. In fact, more years had passed since I had last been in school than most of them were old. Twenty-four years is a long time. I was rusty. I taught students regularly but hadn't formally been on the other side for decades. I didn't feel comfortable about starting. That's when my friend Dianne, the consummate educator, sent me the elephant.

"You must have this," she said. "It brought *me* through; it'll do that for you."

In Divine order, the envelope came in the mail and I fingered the drawing of the largest animal on earth, not as a talisman or a good luck charm, but as a tool. Dear friends like Dianne can answer prayers before you utter them because they know better than you when you really need something. They can feel it in their bones before you can speak it in your spirit.

"I don't know how to take this elephant," I offered.

"One bite at a time," she said. "One bite at a time."

This made sense as I thought about the best way to digest any mammoth thing. Manage it in bits. I studied the two-dimensional 8 ½ by 11 inch paper elephant, lined out with empty blocks. Each block was designed to accommodate one step in my graduate school process. When something is defined, it's amazing how it becomes doable.

I filled in my steps and pinned the drawing on the wall at eye level above my desk, trying not to feel like an anxious child about to begin first grade. But the first time I finished a task on the elephant and rewarded myself by coloring the block, I celebrated. It felt good. It took 36 months to complete my Ph.D. with highest honors. Here are some lessons that I learned on that three-year journey.

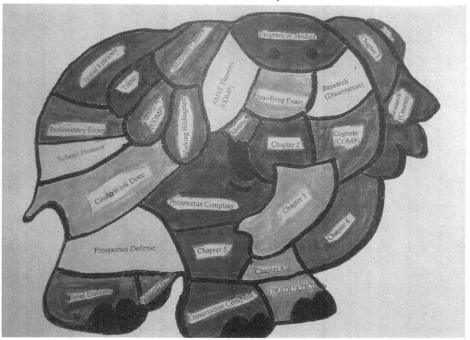

~ Practical Matters: How to Complete the Elephant ~

- Make a list of all steps in *your* graduate studies process (Anything is fair game; i.e., registration, course work, research, proposal writing.)
- Place these steps randomly in blocks on the elephant. You may create as many blocks as you need, in any order. The more you have, the more frequently you will have a chance to color in your spaces.
- As you complete a step, color the block with pen, pencil or crayon of your favorite colors... and then pat yourself on the back.
- Reserve a special block (anywhere on the elephant) for your ultimate reward: "Graduation!"

~ What I Learned About Getting a Degree ~

Anyone who is languishing, hesitating or standing as "ABD" (All But Dissertation) needs an elephant. Here are some tips to motivate those on the verge of making a mature choice to go to school for the first time, to return after time away or to continue once you have paused.

Lesson #1 – It's never too early to start... or to start again.

Once you make a decision to go to school, <u>begin</u>. This is most important so that you don't become discouraged and stop. In my case, I started *seven months* before I entered a classroom. During that lead-up time, I figured out my courses, found copies of the syllabi and interviewed potential professors and fellow students. I bought textbooks and read them on the beach during vacation, in my spare time as I exercised—everywhere. Sometimes I found myself reading the texts in the wrong order. But, at least, the head start calmed my fears, eased my nerves and made me feel like I knew what I was doing. It paid off when I finally started the program. In the first course I took, I was required to read the same 12 books I had already read. By then, the material was familiar.

Lesson #2 – Study what you love.

Nothing can be worse than hating what you're doing or being indifferent to how it unfolds. I made the right choice when I decided to study my passion. I became energized to do the impossible, instantly re-inventing the 24-hour clock and figuring out how to balance life's demands.

When you study something you really want to do or yearn to know more about, you learn how to write from the heart as well as the head. You read from experience as well as the book. You receive theories and concepts and own them with a passion that pushes you to embrace the work intimately.

Lesson #3 – Work smart and avoid the hassle.

At one point, I was stuck. On the day I learned to work smart, I had an "a-ha" moment. It happened when I spotted an opportunity in a class assignment to pair my career life experience with an abstract theory. The former seemed to be a perfect application of the latter. Could it be that I really _did_ something before I knew what it was? In order to work smart, it's wise to:

- Decide on the emphasis of your major research as early as possible.
- Work some aspect of your chosen topic into _every_ paper you write for _every_ class. The repetition is good for your mastery, not to mention that you save time in your research.
- Treat the experience as if you were going to war. Prepare for comprehensive exams and writing of big papers by taking extensive notes. Approach it like boot camp: study, ask questions, scour the information and write. I used 3 x 5 cards for the notes since I wanted to feel the information but a digital record is just as useful. Place the information in easily accessed files. Make hard copies to keep in front of your eyes. Then, voila! Obtuse theories and names, facts and figures are at your fingertips when you need them. This can be a dissertation life raft.
- Don't be selfish: Tutor or mentor somebody else. Inspire them. Give away what you know and you will grow stronger in the process.

Lesson #4 – Stay focused and avoid the hype.

It's easy to get sidetracked, distracted by things that lure you in—department politics, intriguing new disciplines, life moments. Inevitably, right when you are about to study, someone will tempt you to go elsewhere. Resist the temptation to follow a whim or an indulgence, to read emails or answer phone calls. If something is important, boost it in your line of priorities and do it. If it's not important, forget it. Somebody once told me, "The best dissertation is a done dissertation." The idea is to get it done.

A final word...

At my graduation in 1999, I marched in my father's robe. It was the same academic regalia he wore in 1955, when he received his doctorate from Boston University. Dad had died several years before but I felt his spirit in the gown. In every crease and fold, audacity. In every fiber and thread, daring. In every stripe on the sleeve, courage. Wearing the robe felt good. I had taken the risk. I had eaten the elephant. From above, I'm certain my father watched and smiled.

≈

8

The Potter and the Clay

I've never made pottery but a friend once told me about a sculptor he met with a reputation for doing beautiful work. She created gorgeous bowls for serving, vases that seemed to sing on their own, ceramic dishes that made people with houses wish they had enough wall space for hanging. The potter was a genius, everybody said, because her work seemed to laugh and smirk at the same time, bringing to life the most inanimate of objects as healing tools.

The sculptor, originally from somewhere in Southeast Asia, probably came from a tradition of ceramicists who claimed the legacy of 45 centuries of skilled artisans working with clay. She may have even come from China whose name is synonymous with the fine porcelain pieces that grace museums and tables. But her work was different and unique because it seemed to live.

As a veteran who had mastered her art over decades, the sculptor worked with confidence. So when my friend met her, he wasn't surprised that she agreed to allow a small group of art students to watch her step-by-step process. They came to her studio prepared to take notes, intent on learning every detail of how to make their work better. They thought they knew what to expect since they had studied clay carefully. They knew how important it was to get the right kind—either high fire or low fire; they knew that the earthen material had to be rid of the bubbles, which conventional wisdom said had to go; and they knew about centering.

That was the key, they had heard. Centering. Spend time getting *this* right, as the first step, and all else would go well. The proper way to center was to throw the clay onto a stationary wheel, making sure that it hit the dead middle of the hard surface. Even if they had to try repeatedly, they needed to center the clay before turning on the wheel.

But on this day, as the group of neophytes watched, something different happened. They heard a whirring. The clay was not in place; it had not been pounded down. The sculptor had started the wheel and, with more a sense of purpose than abandon, had thrown the clay on as the wheel turned. The clay had a mind of its own, dancing up and down through the sculptor's fingers. Her wet hands touched the substance as if it would run away and sometimes it did. She pushed and pulled. It resisted and finally yielded.

She had skipped a step and had violated a central rule for making perfect ceramic pieces. The students were aghast. One brave soul ventured to ask the question on everybody's mind.

"Why didn't you center the clay first?" The query hung in the air as an unusual calm spread over the space. Something different was unfolding.

The sculptor took a deep breath. Without hesitating, without removing her fingers from the substance she knew and loved, without looking up from the clay that had her complete attention, she responded.

"As long as I am centered, my work always will be."

The students had studied the clay, but on this day they learned how important it is to know the potter. The results are remarkable.

9

More Than A Few Good Men

The speakerphone meant I could hear both sides of the conversation, even though I wasn't in it.

"It's what I have to do," said the voice on the other end.

"You're the man," encouraged my husband Joe sitting in our den.

I recognized the voice of our friend Ellis in California and knew he and Joe must have been talking about some commitment or promise made to any of the dozens of people who depend on them. Ellis had been through a lot. Nine years before, he had supported his wife (my friend Bebe) as she plunged quickly from good health into sickness and found herself making tough choices that no one should have to make. He had nursed her, pampered her and literally lifted her when her fragile body failed. Then when she died, he had taken her daughter from another marriage, her granddaughter and her mother as his own, continuing to love them and act on their behalf.

"You're a good man," I said, sweeping into the room and into the conversation uninvited.

"There are more than a few of us," Ellis replied without hesitation. "Somebody should write about that."

It hit me like a tornado out of nowhere. Nobody much talks about Black men who are good or are doing "good." Much of the news implies that Black men leave their families and responsibilities or cheat or try to beat the system in one way or another. Stories of Black men hauled off in handcuffs depict them as threatening monsters and menaces who generate fear and terror in

43

their wake. And then there are stories about unarmed innocents who die, not because they deserve to get shot in the back, pushed to the ground, strangled with force or dumped in jail, but because somebody did it anyway. Importantly, some of the stories surface from cell phone cameras and in YouTube videos, from reporters' accounts on screens of all sizes. But there are many more stories and many more men who are ignored completely, silent in their living, written out of history as though they never existed.

Who tells about the lives of those ordinary Black men who hustle and flow their way through a tough time, who take the idea of "standing in the gap" literally, who support their partners every day with unconditional love that binds families and heals wounds? Who tells the stories of those mighty men who work, sometimes two jobs, or one with very long double-shift hours or one whenever they can get it, so that someone they care about can eat or study in college or rest a while? Not many people talk about those Black men who are there and present and loving. They do exist.

They are principals and plumbers, dentists and day workers, postal employees and professors, artists and entrepreneurs, bus drivers and bankers who put someone else's welfare before theirs. They direct family travel plans, coach soccer teams and offer advice to wayward youngsters without hesitation or a second request. They are generous. They volunteer in their churches, their fraternities and their community centers; they wash dishes, pay bills, dry tears and fix what's broken. They solve problems while they teach lessons they wish they had learned early on and speak words of encouragement they wish they had heard when they were younger. They live in the heart of the big city, on the edge of the small town, in the middle of the county, at the back of a storefront or on an island not far from most things. They reside in high rises, basement apartments, stately homes, cottages, brownstones, condos, ranch styles, homeless shelters. They are everywhere.

In spite of what people think of them because they've been painted with a single brush; in spite of what they must tell their children about how to survive; in spite of how they must manage every unjust situation they encounter; in spite of getting used to more no's than yes's in matters of business, they stand tall. They are good men who love deeply while they babysit toddlers and chauffeur pre-teens. They are good men who hug their partners and protect their vulnerabilities. They are good men who anchor families with their sacrifices and their souls.

Their lives are common, but their stories are not. In their silence they speak with their actions. Ellis was right. It's up to those who know, to tell.

≈

10

No Red Light in Ty Ty

When people tell you "no" long enough, you believe it. Proclamations of what you can't do can debilitate and inhibit you in a way that is crippling. So that if you come from a family that proclaims "yes" as a way of being in the world, you celebrate. My friend Wilson celebrated from the time he was born, to the time he left Ty Ty. This is a story he remembered.

As a hamlet in Georgia of just over 700 people, Ty Ty boasted farmers.

Wilson's people, men and women, worked the land and kept mules and horses. But they also did something else. In the 1950s and 60s, the town held restrictions, especially for Black people, and set up proverbial fences designed to stand in the way of those planning to excel. But Wilson's grandmother always told him something different about achievement. "Everything is possible," she taught her children and each of her 20 grandchildren in much the same way she monitored the road. People driving through the one main street of the tiny town in Tifton County knew what Wilson's grandmother saw.

"When I was growing up, there was no red light in Ty Ty," said Wilson. "Back then we could be anything."

In her wisdom, Wilson's grandmother could see beyond the corners and the curves. She knew that the only real barriers that could slow her progeny were ones they created themselves. The idea that you set your own limits of how fast you went and when, had been handed down. One generation told the next. What guided you was not an external barrier but an internal flame. What shaped you was not a signal from someone else but values embedded deep in your spirit.

Wilson went to nearby Tifton to a high school named after his uncle who had learned the lessons early. Work hard; be ethical; revere God; love family; treat others fairly; bring somebody else along. And when you do, things will pay off. By the time Wilson finished school and left Ty Ty, he had learned those same lessons. He knew he would go to Morehouse College, meet men like the renowned Benjamin Mays and begin to negotiate traffic signals in places that really did have them. . He joined the ROTC, went to Vietnam where he was wounded and won a Bronze star, had three more tours of duty in Desert Storm and Iraq, became a sergeant major and came home to a quiet life as a distinguished veteran and family man.

On foreign soil, he had been a medic without a weapon—"on point," which means that he had assumed the first and most exposed position in the military formation. He had walked in the most vulnerable place, had taken the most dangerous spot, had been positioned to catch hostile fire. In the process, as he took risks, he had to be alert to save the lives of people he did not know on both sides. Back home he withstood being called names that no one deserved to be called. He heard voices that said, "no" more times than anyone should hear. But he continued to live a life that said, "yes." In so doing, he honored people like Mrs. Flora Mathis, his high school chemistry teacher, who inspired him to think; his six brothers and two sisters who encouraged him to care; and his grandmother who, from the beginning, saw nothing to stop him— not even a red light. Ty Ty lived in his bones.

❦

11

An Open Letter to Our Grandson Little John on Turning 18

July 15, 2015

Dear John:

All of your life, your grandfather and I have called you Little John, but today you are a man. You turn 18 and we pray you will fly. You turn 18 in a world that rubs its hands in anticipation that you will fall apart, make a mistake, do something crazy, even die. You turn 18 in a world that did not expect you to make it to this day. Black boys face perceptions that threaten their bodies and realities that skew their possibilities. They don't get second chances, open doors, the benefit of the doubt, ways around, or many opportunities to shine. You turn 18 and have defied every one of those shortcomings by sheer willpower, by guidance from those who love you, by divine protection, by the Grace of God.

You turn 18 and we do not take it lightly. We are grateful.

You carry in your body the blood of courageous ancestors whose spirits should be ringing in your ears. You carry in your head the memory of a growing-up community whose encouragement should be pulsating in your heart. We pray every day that those two will meet in your soul and help you to search for yourself. That is important so that you can always be part of the conversation.

Once, when you were about five, you asked me, "Nana Judi, what's a conversation?" You were really seeking an answer; truly trying to understand a grown-up world through a child's eyes. I told you in the simplest, most direct way I knew how.

"A conversation is when someone talks and someone listens." You, in your perceptive wisdom responded, "Then *I'll* talk and *you* listen."

As you turn 18, I urge you to participate on both fronts. Talk and listen. Never forget those who by example showed and told you what *not* to do; what *not* to say; what *not* to believe. They too have value.

Never forget the compassion you have found to help a little cousin learn to swim, to aid an aging grandparent negotiate stairs, to comfort a stranger in need, to take a moment to smile.

Never forget those who either did not have the chance to step into manhood or had it cut short by injustice: Michael Brown, Trayvon Martin, Eric Garner, Dontre Hamilton, John Crawford, Tamir Rice, Freddie Gray and so many more. Some were boys who never became men; others were men snatched prematurely from their potential.

As you enter your first year of college, we pray a hedge of protection around you so that you may reach what God has in store for you and so that you may be a part of the conversation—talking and listening. The exchange is necessary. We are proud of the young man you have become and are expecting the mature man you will one day be. We thank God for your life.

Love,
Nana Judi

12

A Few Final Thoughts

I danced on my Daddy's feet and learned to stand on my own. Like so many little 4-year olds, I followed a dream and pretended to fly each time I stepped onto my father's instep. I floated away when he picked up one of his size 11½-D shoes and placed it down again. He wrapped me in his arms and dwarfed me in his love. It was not a childhood fantasy. It was real. We danced to old jazz standards in front of the mirror. I'll never forget. I didn't have to think or decide, just let him do the work. I could spin or waltz, slide or sway— everything was possible just by letting him take charge. It felt good and easy and safe.

The preparation helped me get ready for dancing on my own, for days when he and my Mom wouldn't be around; for times when I would have to make my own decisions. I began this book by claiming to be my mother's child. I am. But just as much, what I have come to understand about life is from my father who insisted that I be grounded in the things God places in your path. Dad passed away before I earned my Ph.D., before we re-built the shed, before Little John was born, before I met Aunt Mae or went to the Virgin Islands or had cancer.

It's been 20 years since he died. Not a day goes by when I don't think of him. But I can hear him as clearly as if I stood on my little-girl toes on his feet. "Keep your eyes open." "Be a quiet force for good." "Don't ever stop learning." "Stay close to the fire but don't jump in." "Have the kind of courage that rattles the soul." "Tell the story of the good folks you know." "Believe in yourself—you're worth it."

Above all, he would say, "Trust God, He's a strong foundation."

My gentile, courageous, button-down collared Dad, who was a stickler for what he called, "the King's English," wouldn't have put it this way, but he would have approved wholeheartedly in saying, "God is good. He Ain't Sleep."

Then Dad would have given me an additional instruction, just in case: "As often as you can, write a note, like your mother would, and pass on what you've learned."

I challenge you to write your own note and pass it on to others. Reflect on your experiences – the people you know, the places you've been. Where in your life have you seen a "God ain't sleep" moment that has taught you something precious? The lesson may not have been for you, but for you to pass on to someone else. If you're hard pressed to think of a time, as Mama would say, "Just live a while." For safe measure, while you look around, keep this book close, just in case. "God ain't sleep."

www.GodAintSleep.com

A Note on the Author

Judi **Moore Latta, Ph.D.**, is a storyteller. An award-winning journalist and professor of Media, Journalism and Film at Howard University, she also served as Executive Director of Communications and Marketing for the University. As a veteran media professional, she has worked in public and commercial broadcasting as a manager, writer and producer. She served as National Public Radio's first education reporter and earned the George Foster Peabody Award as senior producer of the 26-part documentary series *Wade in the Water: African American Sacred Music Traditions.* For dozens of productions, she has received recognition from the Corporation for Public Broadcasting, American Women in Radio and Television, National Education Association, National Association of Black Journalists and National Federation of Community Broadcasters. She lives with her husband in Silver Spring, Maryland.

24861108R00035

Made in the USA
Middletown, DE
08 October 2015